MEATY Main Dishes

Jennifer S. Larson   Photographs by **Brie Cohen**

MILLBROOK PRESS • MINNEAPOLIS

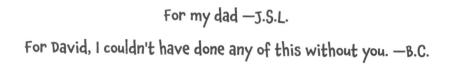

For my dad —J.S.L.

For David, I couldn't have done any of this without you. —B.C.

Photography by Brie Cohen
Food in photographs prepared by chef David Vlach
Illustrations by Laura Westlund/Independent Picture Service
The image on page 5 is used with the permission of © iStockphoto.com/stuartbur.

Allergy alert: The recipes in this book contain ingredients to which some people can be allergic.
Anyone with food allergies or sensitivities should follow the advice of a physician
or other medical professional.

Millbrook Press
A division of Lerner Publishing Group, Inc.
241 First Avenue North
Minneapolis, MN 55401 U.S.A.

Website address: www.lernerbooks.com

Main body text set in Fellbridge Standard.
Typeface provided by Monotype Typography.

Library of Congress Cataloging-in-Publication Data

Larson, Jennifer S., 1967– author.
Meaty main dishes / by Jennifer Larson ; photographs by Brie Cohen.
pages   cm — (You're the chef)
Includes index.
ISBN 978–0–7613–6634–8 (lib. bdg. : alk. paper)
1. Cooking (Meat)—Juvenile literature. 2. Entrees (Cooking)—Juvenile literature.
I. Cohen, Brie, illustrator. II. Title.
TX749.L34 2013
641.82'4—dc23   2012020922

Manufactured in the United States of America
1 – MG – 12/31/12

TABLE of CONTENTS

Are you ready to make some meaty main dishes? YOU can be the chef and make food for yourself and your family. These easy recipes are perfect for a chef who is just learning to cook. And they're so delicious, you'll want to make them again and again!

I developed these recipes with the help of my kids, who are seven and ten years old. They can't do all the cooking on their own yet, but they can do a lot.

Can't get enough of cooking? Check out www.lerneresource.com for bonus recipes, healthful eating tips, links to cooking technique videos, metric conversions, and more!

BEFORE YOU START

Reserve your space! Always ask for permission to work in the kitchen.

Find a helper! You will need an adult helper for some tasks. Talk with this person to decide what steps you can do on your own and what steps the adult will help with.

Make a plan! Read through the whole recipe before you start cooking. Do you have the ingredients you'll need? If you don't know what a certain ingredient is, see page 31 to find out more. Do you understand each step? If you don't understand a technique, such as *drain* or *slice*, turn to page 7. At the beginning of each recipe, you'll see how much time you'll need to prepare the recipe and to cook it. The recipe will also tell you how many servings it makes. Small drawings at the top of each recipe let you know what major kitchen equipment you'll need—such as a stovetop, a toaster, or a microwave.

stovetop

toaster

knives

microwave

oven

Wash up! Always wash your hands with soap and water before you start cooking. And wash them again after you touch raw eggs, meat, or fish.

Get it together! Find the tools you'll use, such as measuring cups or a mixing bowl. Gather all the ingredients you'll need. That way you won't have to stop to look for things once you start cooking.

SAFETY TIPS

That's sharp! Your adult helper needs to be in the kitchen when you are using a knife, a grater, or a peeler. If you are doing the cutting, use a cutting board. Cut away from your body, and keep your fingers away from the blade.

That's hot! Be sure an adult is in the kitchen if you use the stove or the oven. Your adult helper can help you cook on the stove and take hot things out of the oven.

Tie it back! If you have long hair, tie it back or wear a hat. If you have long sleeves, roll them up. You want to keep your hair and clothing out of the food and away from flames or other heat sources.

Turn that handle! When cooking on the stove, turn the pot handle toward the back. That way, no one will accidentally bump the pot and knock it off the stove.

Finish the job right!

One of your most important jobs as a chef is to clean up when you're done. Wash the dishes with soap and warm water. Wipe off the countertop or table. Put away any unused ingredients. The adults in your house will be more excited for you to cook next time if you take charge of cleaning up.

Wash it! If you are working with raw eggs or meat, you need to keep things extra clean. After cutting raw meat or fish, wash the knife and cutting board right away. They must be clean before you use them to cut anything else.

Go slowly! Take your time when you're working. When you are doing something for the first time, such as peeling or grating, be sure not to rush.

Above all, have fun!

COOKING TOOLS

baking pans

bowls

broiler pan

can opener

colander

cookie sheet

cutting board

dish towel

dry measuring cups

fork

frying pan

grater

knives

large spoon

liquid measuring cup

measuring spoons

oven mitt

serrated knife

skewers

spatula

tongs

wok

wooden spoon

TECHNIQUES

bake: to cook in the oven

boil: to heat liquid on a stovetop until it starts to bubble

chop: to cut food into small pieces using a knife

cover: to put a lid on a pan or pot containing food

discard: to throw away or put in a compost bin. Discarded parts of fruits and vegetables and eggshells can be put in a compost bin, if you have one.

drain: to pour the liquid off of a food. You can drain food by pouring it into a colander or strainer. If you are draining water or juice from canned food, you can also use the lid to hold the food back while the liquid pours out.

grate: to use a food grater to shred food into small pieces

mix: to stir food using a spoon or fork

preheat: to turn the oven to the temperature you will need for baking. An oven takes about 15 minutes to heat up.

puree: to blend until smooth

serrated: a tool, such as a knife, that has a bumpy edge

set aside: to put nearby in a bowl or plate or on a clean workspace

shred: to cut or grate into small pieces

simmer: to boil at a low heat setting. The liquid will be boiling with very tiny bubbles.

slice: to cut food into thin pieces

sprinkle: to scatter on top

MEASURING

To measure **dry ingredients**, such as sugar or flour, spoon the ingredient into a measuring cup until it is full. Then use the back of a table knife to level it off. Do not pack it down unless the recipe tells you to. Do not use measuring cups made for liquids.

When you're measuring a **liquid**, such as milk or water, use a clear glass or plastic measuring cup. Set the cup on the table or a counter, and pour the liquid into the cup. Pour slowly and stop when the liquid has reached the correct line.

Don't measure your ingredients over the bowl they will go into. If you accidentally spill, you might have way too much!

serves 4 to 6

preparation time: 20 minutes
cooking time: 20 to 25 minutes

ingredients:

2 green onions
16 ounces lean ground turkey
2 tablespoon Parmesan cheese
½ teaspoon oregano
1 teaspoon salt
freshly ground black pepper
1 tablespoon vegetable oil
6 hamburger buns
condiments such as ketchup,
    mustard, mayonnaise, lettuce,
    and avocado slices

equipment:

cutting board
knife
medium bowl
measuring spoons
large fork
9 x 13 inch baking pan (or other
    baking pan with sides)
oven mitts
spatula

Meat is a great way to get protein, an essential part of our diet. But we don't need to eat a lot of meat to get the protein we need. Make sure to eat plenty of fruits and vegetables too!

Terrific Turkey Burgers

Cook these delicious burgers in the oven.
Or grill them outdoors for a summer picnic.
Have an adult help you with the baking or grilling.

1. Preheat the oven to 350°F.

2. **Wash** the green onions. Next, use a knife and a cutting board to **cut** off the roots and discard. Remove any dry or wilted green parts. Then **slice** the onions into small pieces about ½ inch long. You can use both the white and green parts of the onion.

3. **Place** the turkey in a mixing bowl. **Add** green onions, Parmesan cheese, oregano, salt, and pepper. **Mix** together with a fork.

4. Pour vegetable oil into a baking pan. Use a spatula or your clean fingers to **spread** the oil around.

5. Use your (clean) hands to make the turkey into patties. **Divide** the mixture into 6 balls. (If you want bigger burgers, you can make just 4 patties.) The balls should be all the same size. **Flatten** and **shape** each ball into a round, flat patty. Lay the patties in the baking pan. They should be spaced so they are not touching. **Wash** your hands after making the patties.

6. Use oven mitts to **put** the pan in the oven. Bake at 350°F for 20 to 25 minutes, or until cooked through. To check if they are done, use oven mitts to **remove** the pan from the oven, and set the pan on top of the stove. **Cut** 1 burger in half. If it is still pink in the middle, put the pan back in the oven for another 3 to 5 minutes.

7. **Remove** the burgers with a spatula. **Serve** on hamburger buns. **Top** with the condiments you like.

TRY THIS!
Get creative with your toppings. Try strips of red or green peppers, shredded carrots, or cucumber slices. Or experiment with your favorite salad dressing.

serves 3 to 6

preparation time: 15 minutes
(plus 60 minutes for chicken
to marinate)
cooking time: 45 to 50 minutes

ingredients:

1 lemon
1 teaspoon fresh or dried
   rosemary
2 tablespoons olive oil or
   vegetable oil
½ teaspoon garlic powder
6 chicken drumsticks
salt and pepper

equipment:

9 x 9 inch baking pan (or other
   baking pan)
large spoon
cutting board
knife
measuring spoons
paper towels
plastic wrap
oven mitts
hot pad

When you're at
the store buying meat,
you might see items that
say "free-range chicken."
What does that mean? Free-
range chickens are not raised
in cages and are free to
go outside.

Juicy Chicken Drumsticks

Impress your family with this recipe for baked chicken drumsticks. Serve the drumsticks alongside a vegetable and some fruit, and you will have a hearty meal.

1. On a cutting board, **cut** the lemon in half. **Squeeze** ½ lemon into a small bowl to get the juice out. You will need to **scoop** out the seeds with a small spoon. Repeat with the other half.

2. If you are using fresh rosemary, **wash** it under cool water. **Pull** the little rosemary leaves (they look like pine needles) off the stem. Put the rosemary leaves onto a cutting board and push them into a little pile. Use the knife to **chop** the piled leaves into smaller pieces. If you are using dried rosemary, you can **crumble** it in your hands to make smaller pieces.

3. **Put** lemon juice, olive oil, garlic powder, and rosemary in the baking pan. **Mix** with a spoon. This mixture is the marinade.

4. Take the chicken out of the package. Remove 1 drumstick and **rinse** it under cool water to clean it. **Pat** it dry with a paper towel, and **place** it in the baking pan. Repeat with the other drumsticks. **Wash** your hands when you are done handling the uncooked chicken.

5. Use the spoon to **pour** some marinade on top of each drumstick. **Sprinkle** the drumsticks with salt and pepper.

6. **Cover** the pan of chicken with a piece of plastic wrap. **Put** the chicken in the refrigerator for an hour.

7. **Preheat** the oven to 350°F.

8. Use oven mitts to put the baking pan in the oven. **Bake** the chicken for 45 to 50 minutes, or until done. To check if the chicken is done, use oven mitts to take the baking pan out of the oven. **Cut** near the bone of a piece of chicken. If it is still pink in the center, put it back in the oven for another 5 to 10 minutes. **Place** the pan on a hot pad. Serve.

serves 4 to 6

preparation time: 15 minutes
cooking time: 25 to 30 minutes

ingredients:

1 small onion
1 carrot
1 egg
1 pound lean ground beef
2 tablespoons taco seasoning
  mix
salt and pepper
salsa or guacamole (optional)

equipment:

cutting board
knife
measuring cup—¼ cup
small bowl
fork
large bowl
mixing spoon (or fork)
aluminum foil
1 cookie sheet
small spoon
oven mitts
spatula
plate
toothpicks (optional)

Flavorful
Taco Meatballs

Serve some meatballs with a bit of Mexican flavor
for dinner or for a snack.

1. **Preheat** the oven to 375°F.

2. **Cut** off both ends of the onion. Set the onion on one
of the flat parts you made by cutting it. Cut the onion
in half. **Wrap** one half in plastic wrap, and store it for
another time. **Peel** off and discard the papery
layers around the outside of the other
half. Lay the onion half flat
on the cutting board. **Cut**
the onion crosswise into
semicircular slices. Then
chop the slices into small
pieces. Cut enough to make
¼ cup. Set aside.

3. **Wash** the carrot in cool water. Use a knife and cutting board to cut off and discard the top and bottom. Use a grater to **grate** 2 tablespoons of carrot.

4. In a small bowl, **crack** the egg and beat it slightly with a fork.

5. Put the onion, carrot, egg, ground beef, and taco seasoning in a large bowl. **Add** a shake of salt and pepper. **Mix** together with a mixing spoon or a fork.

6. Put a sheet of aluminum foil on your cookie sheet. Use a small spoon to **scoop** out a glob of meatball mixture. **Roll** the mixture between your (clean) hands. The meatball should be about 1 inch wide. Place the finished meatball on the foil. Repeat this step until you've used all the meatball mixture. **Wash** your hands when you are done handling the uncooked meatballs.

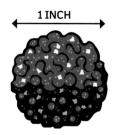

1 INCH

7. Use oven mitts to **put** the cookie sheet in the oven. Bake 25 to 30 minutes. Use oven mitts to **remove** the sheet from the oven. Put the sheet on the stovetop. Meatballs should be brown all the way through. To check if they are done, you can **cut** a meatball in half to see if it is brown on the inside. If the inside is still pink, put the cookie sheet back in the oven for 2 to 3 minutes and check again.

8. Use a spatula to **transfer** the meatballs from the cookie sheet to a plate. You can stick a toothpick in each meatball and serve them that way. **Dip** in salsa or guacamole if desired.

serves 4

preparation time: 10 minutes
cooking time: 10 to 15 minutes

ingredients:

1 lemon
1 pound fish (sole, flounder, cod, or haddock are good choices)
½ teaspoon dried dill (or 1 teaspoon fresh dill)
½ teaspoon salt
pepper

equipment:

9 x 13 inch baking pan
cutting board
knife
aluminum foil
measuring spoons
oven mitts

Easy Baked Fish

Did you know that baked fish is simple to make and healthy too?

1. **Preheat** the oven to 400°F.

2. Use a knife and cutting board to **cut** the lemon in half. **Squeeze** the ½ lemon into a small bowl to get the juice out. You will need to **scoop** out the seeds with a small spoon. Repeat with the other half.

3. **Tear off** a piece of foil big enough to fit in the baking sheet and have extra room to fold over the top of the fish. **Place** it in the bottom of the pan.

4. Take the fish out of the package. **Rinse** it under cold water to clean it, and pat it dry with a paper towel. **Place** it in the pan. **Wash** your hands when you are done handling the fish.

5. **Pour** the lemon juice on top of the fish. **Sprinkle** the dill and salt on top. **Add** 1 or 2 sprinkles of pepper.

6. **Fold** the foil over the top of the fish. Use oven mitts to **put** the baking pan in the oven.

7. **Bake** for about 15 minutes. To **check** if the fish is done, use oven mitts to **remove** the baking pan from the oven. Be careful when you **open** the foil, as hot steam will come out. With a clean fork, **test** the fish to see if it easily comes apart in flakes. If it does flake, it is done. If it's not done, put it in the oven for 2 to 3 minutes and check again.

TRY THIS!

Try other herbs instead of dill, such as **oregano** or **basil**.

You can also put vegetables on top of the fish before cooking, such as **tomato** or **zucchini** slices.

serves 4 to 6

preparation time: 15 minutes
(plus 60 minutes for shrimp to
thaw)
cooking time: 15 to 20 minutes

ingredients:

1 pound frozen, deveined
   shrimp with tails removed
1 tablespoon vegetable oil
1 pound bag frozen stir-fry
   vegetables (sometimes you
   can find some labeled Asian
   stir fry. Otherwise, look for a
   mixture of peapods, peppers,
   broccoli, and onion.)
½ teaspoon garlic powder
1 3-ounce package ramen
   noodle soup
2 tablespoons soy sauce
1 teaspoons ground ginger
2 tablespoons water

equipment:

gallon size zip-top plastic bag
large bowl
spatula
measuring spoons
knife
liquid measuring cup
large frying pan or wok
wooden spoon
medium saucepan
colander
small bowl
spoon

Asian Shrimp Stir Fry

Impress your family with this delicious
shrimp and vegetable stir fry.

1. **Place** the unopened shrimp
   package in a zip-top bag and close
   the bag tightly. Place the bag of
   shrimp in a big bowl in the sink.
   Run cold water over the shrimp
   until the bowl is full. Let the shrimp
   sit in the bowl to thaw. It will take
   about 1 hour.

2. **Pour** the vegetable oil in the frying pan. Turn the
   burner under the pan on medium high. Remove
   the thawed shrimp from its package
   and **add** it to the pan.
   Sometimes oil can spatter
   out of the pan when cooking.
   Watch out! Cook for 3 to 5 minutes,
   turning the shrimp with a spatula.
   The shrimp is done when
   it is pink. **Remove** the
   shrimp from the pan and
   place them on a plate. Set
   aside.

3. **Put** the frozen vegetables into the pan. Measure the
   garlic powder and **add** it to the vegetables. **Stir**, then
   cover the pan. Cook until vegetables are hot, about 5
   minutes. Turn off the burner and leave the pan there.

4. Measure 2 cups of water and **pour** in a saucepan. **Cover** the saucepan with a lid, and turn the burner under the saucepan to high. **Heat** the water until boiling.

5. **Open** the package of ramen noodle soup and discard the flavor packet. Have an adult help you **put** the noodles into the boiling water. Cook for 3 minutes, **stirring** with a wooden spoon once or twice.

6. When noodles are done cooking, have an adult **drain** them into a colander. **Add** the noodles and the shrimp to the vegetables in the frying pan.

7. In a small bowl, **mix** the soy sauce, ginger, and 2 tablespoons water with a spoon. **Pour** the mixture over the shrimp and vegetables. Serve.

TRY THIS!
You can use chicken, beef, or tofu instead of shrimp.

17

Hot Dog People

Have fun making a face, hair, and clothes on a hot dog person you can eat!

serves 4

preparation time: 15 minutes
cooking time: 5 minutes

ingredients:
4 hot dogs
4 slices wheat bread
ketchup
mustard
alfalfa sprouts (optional)
lettuce

equipment:
cutting board
knife
medium saucepan
tongs
toaster (optional)

1. **Place** a hot dog on the cutting board. Starting at the halfway point, **cut** down the middle of the hot dog all the way to the bottom. These are the legs.

2. Make a short **cut** on one side of the hot dog about a third of the way down from the top. Then make the same cut on the other side. These are the arms.

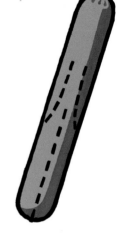

3. **Repeat** steps 1 and 2 for the rest of the hot dogs.

4. **Fill** a saucepan about halfway with water. Turn the burner under the saucepan to high. When the water is boiling, have an adult help you use tongs to **place** the hot dogs in the water. Boil for 5 minutes, or until the arms and legs open up.

5. Use tongs to **place** each hot dog person on a piece of bread. **Make** a face at the top with ketchup and mustard. Use the alfalfa sprouts to make hair. Use the lettuce to make clothes. Serve on toasted wheat bread.

serves 4

preparation time: 10 to 15
  minutes
cooking time: 3 minutes

ingredients:

1 apple
½ stalk celery
2 3-ounce cans tuna packed in
  water
2 tablespoons mayonnaise
½ teaspoon curry powder
  (optional)
4 slices whole wheat bread

equipment:

can opener
cutting board
knife
measuring spoons
medium bowl
spoon
toaster

TRY THIS!

Try serving this in a **cucumber boat** instead of on toast. Cut a medium cucumber in half the long way. Use a spoon to scoop out the seeds on each half. Fill the boat with tuna filling.

Tangy Tuna on Toast

This light and crunchy tuna meal is great for a quick snack or dinner on a hot day. Try adding the curry powder for a tangy twist.

1. **Wash** the apple and celery in cool water.

2. To cut the apple, first **cut** it in half from top to bottom. Take a half and cut it in half again from top to bottom. Then cut out and **discard** the stem and seeds. **Chop** into pieces. Repeat these steps with the other half. Put apple pieces in a medium bowl.

3. To cut the celery, first **cut** off any leaves or wilted parts. Then cut off the bottom edge. Cut the celery in half lengthwise so you have 2 long strips. Then **slice** each strip into small chunks. Cut enough for 2 tablespoons of celery. Put the celery in the bowl with the apple.

4. To drain the tuna, **open** the can with a can opener. Hold the top circle of metal in place while you **tilt** the can to the side. Let the liquid **drain** into the sink. Be careful not to touch the sharp edge of the cut metal circle.

5. **Add** the tuna, mayonnaise, and curry powder to the apple and celery. **Mix** the ingredients together with a spoon.

6. **Put** the bread in the toaster. When the toast is done, take it out carefully. Put each piece of toast on a plate.

7. **Spread** ¼ of the tuna mixture on each piece of toast. Enjoy.

serves 4 to 5

preparation time: 15 to 20 minutes
(plus 60 minutes for chicken to
marinate)
cooking time: 25 to 30 minutes

ingredients:

1 lemon
4 tablespoons olive oil or
    vegetable oil
1 teaspoon Italian seasoning
½ teaspoon salt
pepper
1 pound chicken breasts
1 green or red pepper
1 small zucchini
5 to 6 mushrooms (optional)
1 medium onion

equipment:

knife
cutting board
medium bowl
small bowl
spoon
paper towel
plastic wrap or a plate
8 metal or wooden skewers
pan for soaking wooden skewers
oven mitts
broiler pan (pan that fits in the
    broiler of your oven) or cookie
    sheet

Fancy Chicken Kebabs

Serve these kebabs for a fancy—and tasty—meal!

1. Use a knife and cutting
board to **cut** the lemon
in half. **Squeeze** the ½
lemon into a medium bowl
to get the juice out. You
will need to **scoop** out the
seeds with a small spoon.
Repeat with the other half.

2. **Put** olive or vegetable oil, Italian seasoning, salt,
and a few shakes of pepper in the bowl. **Stir** with a
spoon. This is the marinade. Place 3 tablespoons of
marinade in a separate bowl. You will pour this over
the vegetables later. Set aside both bowls.

3. Take the chicken out of the package.
Rinse it under cool water, and pat it
dry with a paper towel. Place it on a
cutting board. **Cut** a piece of chicken
lengthwise into 1-inch strips. Then cut
the strips into 1-inch pieces. Repeat
with the rest of the chicken. Be sure
to **wash** the cutting board and
knife with hot, soapy water
before cutting anything else
with them. And wash your
hands too!

4. **Place** the chicken pieces in a medium bowl, and **spoon** the marinade over them. **Cover** the bowl with plastic wrap or a plate. Put the chicken in the refrigerator. Leave to marinate for 1 hour.

5. If you are using wooden skewers, they need to soak for an hour too. **Place** them in a pan and **cover** them with water.

Turn the page for more Fancy Chicken Kebabs

6. **Wash** the green or red pepper, zucchini, and mushrooms in cool water. Use the knife and a clean cutting board to cut the vegetables. To **cut** the pepper, start by cutting around the stem. Then cut the green pepper in half and **remove** the seeds. Discard the stem and seeds. **Chop** the rest of the green pepper into 1-inch pieces. Set aside.

7. To cut the zucchini, first **cut** off the stem. Then cut the zucchini into round slices ½ inch thick.

8. **Cut** big mushrooms in half. Smaller mushrooms can be left whole.

9. **Cut** off both ends of the onion. Set the onion on one of the flat parts you made by cutting it. Cut the onion in half. **Peel** off and discard the papery layers around the outside. Lay an onion half flat on the cutting board. **Cut** the onion lengthwise into 2 quarters, separate each quarter into 2 chunks. Repeat with the other half. Set aside.

10. **Preheat** the broiler of your oven to high. Or if you are cooking on an outdoor grill, ask an adult to help get the grill ready.

11. Take the chicken out of the refrigerator. With clean hands, **take** a chunk of meat and carefully **push** it onto the skewer. Make sure your fingers are not in the way, so you don't get poked! Push the chunk all the way to the bottom of the skewer. Repeat this until the skewer is full of chicken pieces close together. Then place the rest of the chicken on other skewers. **Wash** your hands when you are done handling the chicken.

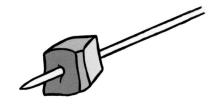

12. **Push** a mixture of vegetables onto a skewer until it is full. You can make a pattern, putting on a pepper, then an onion, then a zucchini, then another pepper, and so on. Put the rest of the vegetables on other skewers.

13. With a spoon, **pour** the marinade you set aside earlier onto the vegetables.

14. Use oven mitts to **put** the skewers on a broiler pan or cookie sheet in the oven (or on the grill). Cook for 15 to 20 minutes. Ask an adult to help you **turn** the skewers once or twice while they are cooking. To check if the chicken is done, use an oven mitt to **take out** 1 skewer. Take off a piece of chicken. **Cut** it to be sure it is not still pink inside. If it's not done, put the skewer back in the oven or grill for 2 to 3 minutes. The vegetables may need less time to cook than the chicken. They are done when they are a little brown and you can easily stick a fork into them. Some people prefer to mix the chicken and vegetables together on the skewers. If you want to do this, be sure to cook the kebabs until the meat is done. The vegetables might become slightly blackened and crisp.

serves 4

preparation time: 10 to 15 minutes
cooking time: 0 minutes

ingredients:

2 medium tomatoes
3 large lettuce leaves
1 carrot
2 pickles
4 whole wheat tortillas
⅓ pound deli meat—can be turkey, roast beef, ham, or some of each
1 package of sliced cheese

condiments:

ranch dressing
mayonnaise
mustard

equipment:

dish towel
knife
cutting board
grater
toothpicks

Deli Meat Rollups

You can make these rolled-up sandwiches for a picnic. Or take one in your school lunch.

1. **Wash** the tomatoes, lettuce, and carrot under cool water. **Dry** the lettuce with a clean dish towel.

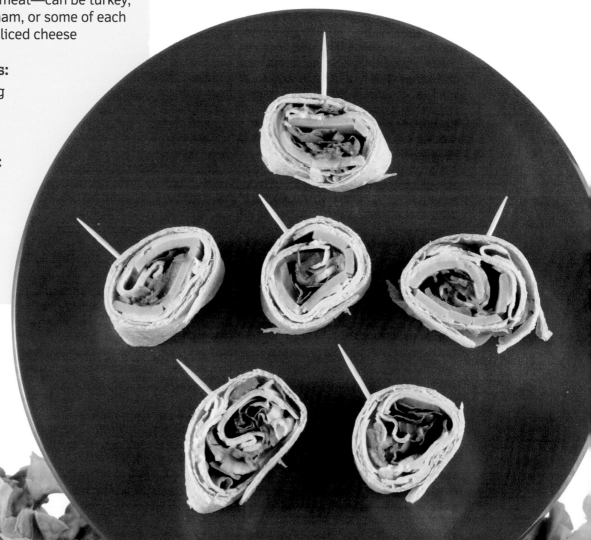

2. Use the knife and cutting board to cut the vegetables. It works best to cut a tomato with a serrated knife, which is a knife with bumps along the sharp edge. To cut the tomato, first cut out the brown circle on the top. Discard it. Then **chop** the rest of the tomato. Set aside.

3. **Place** the lettuce leaves on the cutting board on top of each other. **Roll** them up, tightly all together. **Cut** the roll into slices. After you cut the roll, cut slices of lettuce into smaller pieces.

4. **Cut** the top off the carrot and discard. Use a grater to **grate** about 3 tablespoons of carrot. Set aside.

5. **Cut** the pickles lengthwise into thin slices.

6. **Place** a tortilla on a plate. **Put** 2 to 3 pieces of deli meat on top, covering most of the tortilla.

7. Now comes the fun part. **Add** some toppings to your rolled-up sandwich. Maybe you'll have 1 or 2 slices of cheese, a sprinkle of carrots and lettuce, and top it off with tomatoes and pickles. **Add** 1 or more condiments if you like, such as a squirt of ranch dressing or some mayonnaise or mustard.

8. Now **roll** up your sandwich (if you didn't fill it too full!). You can eat it whole or **slice** it into smaller circles. Stick toothpicks through the tortilla to hold the circles together.

serves 4

preparation time: 15 to 20 minutes
cooking time: 40 to 45 minutes

ingredients:

2 tablespoons ketchup
2 tablespoon vinegar (red wine
   vinegar or white vinegar)
2 tablespoons water
1 teaspoon Worcestershire sauce
¼ teaspoon salt
a few shakes of pepper
5 to 6 small potatoes or 2 to 3
   larger potatoes
3 carrots
1 medium onion
1 pound beef stew meat

equipment:

measuring spoons
measuring cup—1 cup
small bowl
aluminum foil
cutting board
knife
paper towels
9 x 13 inch baking pan
oven mitts

Let's Go Camping Stew

If you're going camping, you can make packets of tasty stew right in the campfire! Or you can pretend you're camping and make them in the oven. You could even have a picnic dinner on your living room floor.

1. **Preheat** the oven to 350°F. (Unless you actually are camping. Then you'll need an adult to help you get your fire ready.)

2. **Measure** the ketchup, vinegar, water, and Worcestershire sauce into a small bowl. **Add** salt and pepper. **Mix** all the ingredients well. This will be the marinade.

3. **Wash** the potatoes and carrots in cool water.

4. Use the knife and cutting board to cut vegetables. To cut a potato, first **slice** it into 1/2-inch circles. Then **chop** each slice into 1/2-inch pieces. Cut enough to make about 2 cups of potatoes.

5. **Cut** the bottom and top off each carrot. Cut each carrot into ½-inch circles. Set them aside.

6. **Cut** off both ends of the onion. Set the onion on one of the flat parts you made by cutting it. Cut the onion in half. **Peel** off and discard the papery layers around the outside. Lay the onion half flat on the cutting board. **Cut** the onion lengthwise into 2 quarters, separate each quarter into 2 chunks. Repeat with the other half. Set aside.

Turn the page for more Let's Go Camping Stew

TRY THIS!

You can make these with **chicken** or **fish**—or no meat at all.

Try adding some different vegetables that you like. **Peppers, mushrooms,** and some **garlic** would be tasty.

7. **Remove** the stew meat from its package. **Wash** it under cool water, and pat it dry with a paper towel. Stew meat often comes already chopped up. If not, **chop** it into 1-inch pieces. **Wash** your hands when you are done handling the raw meat.

8. **Cut** 4 pieces of foil for the stew packets. Each piece should be about 12 inches long. **Place** about 4 to 5 pieces of meat and a handful of vegetables in the center of each piece of foil. Don't fill it too full, or you won't be able to fold it up. **Pour** 1 or 2 tablespoons of marinade over the top.

9. Take 2 opposite sides of the foil and **press** them together above the food. **Fold** them over 2 times to make a seal. Then tightly fold the other 2 edges over the food to completely seal in. Be sure there are no holes—the food will cook better if the steam doesn't escape. (If you are cooking these over a camp fire, wrap each packet in another layer of foil.)

10. **Put** the packets in a baking pan to catch any juices that might leak out. Use oven mitts to **place** the pan in the oven. If you are cooking these over a fire, an adult can help you put the packets on a grill above the fire, or right in the coals.

11. **Bake** for about 40 to 45 minutes, until meat is cooked through and vegetables are tender.

SPECIAL INGREDIENTS

avocado: a large, egg-shaped fruit with dark green bumpy or smooth skin, bright green flesh, and a large pit. Avocados can be found in the produce section of grocery stores.

beef stew meat: beef that is precut into chunks for making stew. You can find packages of this type of beef in most grocery stores. If you can't find beef that is already cut into pieces, you can buy beef and chop it.

herb: a plant used to flavor cooking. Basil, oregano, mint, dill, and rosemary are examples of herbs. You can find dried herbs in the spice section of the grocery store. Many grocery stores and farmers' markets have fresh herbs. Or you can grow your own in the garden or in a pot!

ginger: a root used as a spice. You can find ground ginger in the spice section of the grocery store. Or you can find the fresh root in the produce section. Store fresh ginger in the refrigerator or in the freezer in a bag. Frozen ginger can be grated without thawing.

guacamole: a dip made from ripe avocados. Many stores sell guacamole in the produce section.

salsa: a sauce that may contain tomatoes, hot peppers, garlic, and herbs. It is often used to flavor Mexican dishes and can be found near the chips in the snack food aisle of the grocery store.

shrimp: a type of small seafood. Frozen shrimp can be found in the freezer section of the grocery store. You can purchase it with the shell or peeled and deveined.

soy sauce: a salty sauce often used in Chinese and Japanese dishes. Look for it in the ethnic foods section of most grocery stores.

taco seasoning: a packet of spices blended for tacos. Look for taco seasoning in the grocery store—often near the taco shells and salsa.

Worcestershire sauce: sauce used for adding flavor to meat. It comes in a bottle in the grocery store.

FURTHER READING AND WEBSITES

ChooseMyPlate.gov
http://www.choosemyplate.gov/children
-over-five.html
Download coloring pages, play an
interactive computer game, and get
lots of nutrition information at this U.S.
Department of Agriculture website.

Chop Chop
http://www.chopchopmag.org/
You'll find lots of family-friendly recipes at
this cooking website.

Farmers Markets Search
http://apps.ams.usda.gov/FarmersMarkets/
Find a farmers' market near you!

Graimes, Nicola. *Kids' Fun and Healthy
Cookbook*. New York: DK, 2007.

This cookbook combines tasty recipes with
information about nutrition and healthy
eating habits.

Seafood Watch
http://www.montereybayaquarium.org/cr
/cr_seafoodwatch/sfw_recommendations
.aspx?c=ln
Some seafood is farmed or caught in ways
that harm our rivers, lakes, and oceans. Visit
this website to learn which types of seafood
are best to buy and which should be avoided.

INDEX